New York Dispensary

**Nomenclature and pharmacopoeia of the New York Dispensary**

New York Dispensary

**Nomenclature and pharmacopoeia of the New York Dispensary**

ISBN/EAN: 9783742819154

Manufactured in Europe, USA, Canada, Australia, Japa

Cover: Foto ©Suzi / pixelio.de

Manufactured and distributed by brebook publishing software
(www.brebook.com)

New York Dispensary

# Nomenclature and pharmacopoeia of the New York Dispensary

# NOMENCLATURE

AND

# PHARMACOPŒIA

OF THE

## NEW YORK DISPENSARY.

# LIST OF DISEASES.*

4. Abortion.

1. Abscess.

| | | |
|---|---|---|
| 1. | " | alveolar. |
| 1. | " | fœcal. |
| 1. | " | ischio-rectal. |
| 1. | " | lachrymal. |
| 1. | " | lumbar. |
| 1,4. | " | of brain. |
| 1. | " | " breast. |
| 1. | " | " bone. |
| 1. | " | " bursa. |
| 4. | " | " liver. |
| 2. | " | " lung. |
| 1. | " | " meatus auditorius. |
| 2. | " | " mediastinum. . |
| 3. | " | " prostate. |
| 1,3. | " | " testis. |
| 1,3. | " | " vulva. |

---

* This list is thought to embrace every disease and injury likely to be presented for treatment at the Dispensary, but any case for which it does not give a name may be returned under the name given in the nomenclature of the Royal College of Physicians, a copy of which will be found in the House Physician's room. The numerals at the left-hand side of the page denote the classes to which the various diseases may properly belong—thus, 1 means *Surgery* ; 2, *Heart and Lungs* ; 3, *Venereal and Cutaneous Diseases* ; 4, *Head and Abdomen and Diseases of Women* ; 5, *Children and Unclassified*.

1,4. Abscess, pelvic.

1.   "   pharyngeal.

1.   "   psoas.

1.   "   sub-fascial.

4.   "   sub-peritoneal.

1.   "   thecal.

1,3.   "   urinary.

1. Acne ciliaris.

3.   "   simplex.

3.   "   rosacea.

4. Addison's disease.

4. Adhesion, peritoneal.

1.   "   thecal.

4. Agalactia.

5. Alcoholism.

1. Amaurosis.

1. Amblyopia.

4. Amenorrhœa.

5. Anæmia.

1,5. Anæsthesia of a part.

5. Anasarca.

1,5. Anchyloglossum (olophonia).

1. Anchylosis.

1,2,4. Aneurism.

2.   "   of aorta.

1.   "   traumatic.

1.   "   varicose.

2. Angina pectoris.

1,5.   "   trachealis.

1. Anthrax.

1. Aphonia.
5. Apthæ parasiticæ.
4. Apoplexy.
1. Arthritis.
1.     "     suppurative.
4. Ascites.
2. Asphyxia.
1. Asthenopia.
2. Asthma.
1. Astigmatism.
5. Ataxia, progressive locomotor.
5. Atelcetasis.
5. Atrophy, progressive museular.
1. Avulsion of a part.

3. Balanitis.
3. Balano-posthitis.
4,5. Bile-duct, catarrh of.
4,5.     "     stricture of.
3. Bladder, catarrh of.
1.     "     inversion of.
3.     "     irritable.
3,5.     "     paralysis of.
3. Blennorrhagia.
3. Blennorrhœa.
1,5. Blepharitis.
1,5. Brain, compression of.
1,5.     "     concussion of.
1,5.     "     injury of.
4.     "     softening of.

4. Bright's disease.

4,5.  "        "   acute.

2,5. Bronchitis, acute.

2,5.      "      capillary.

2,5.      "      chronic.

2,5.      "      morbillosa.

1. Bronchocele.

2.     "      exophthalmic.

1. Bursa, enlarged.

1. Byrsitis.


4. Calculus, biliary.

1.     "      prostatic.

4.     "      renal.

1.     "      salivary.

1.     "      urethral.

1.     "      vesical.

1. Cancer.

4.     "      colloid.

1.     "      epithelial.

1.     "      medullary.

1.     "      melanotic.

1.     "      of breast.

4.     "      of stomach.

1.     "      of testis.

4.     "      of uterus.

1.     "      osteoid.

1.     "      scirrhous.

4.     "      villous.

1. Caries.

1. Cartilage, loose.

1. Cataract.

4. Catarrh, acute uterine.

2.    "       bronchial.

1.    "       chronic nasal.

4.    "       chronic uterine.

1.    "       laryngeal.

1. Cellulitis.

1.    "       erysipeloid.

4.    "       pelvic.

1,5. Cephalæmatoma.

1. Cerumen, retained.

3. Chancroid.

3.    "       phagedenic.

3.    "       serpiginous.

3.    "       sloughing.

4. Chlorosis.

4. Cholera Asiatica.

5.    "       infantum.

4.    "       simplex (cholera morbus.)

5. Chorea, acute.

5.    "       chronic.

1. Choroiditis.

4. Cirrhosis

1,4. Coccyodynia.

3. Colpitis.

3. Condyloma.

4. Constipation.

1. Constriction of a part.

1. Contracted fascia.

1,5. Contracted muscle.

1. " tendon.

1. Contusion.

1. Cornea cacuminata.

1. Coryza.

5. Cyanosis.

1,5. Cynanche maligna (angina putris.)

5. " parotidea.

1,5. " tonsillaris.

5. " trachealis.

1. Cystitis, acute.

1,3. " blennorrhagic.

1,3. " chronic.

1. Cystocele.


1. Dacryoadenitis.

1. Dacryocystitis.

5. Debility.

5. Delirium tremens.

5. Dentition.

3. Dermatitis, erysipeloid.

3. " toxica.

5. Diabetes.

4. Diarrhœa.

1. Diastasis.

5. Diphtheria.

1. Diplopia.

1. Dislocation at elbow.

" at hip.

" at knee.

1. Dislocation at shoulder.
  "   at wrist.
  "   of acromial end of clavicle.
  "   of astragalus.
     of costal cartilage.
  "   of foot at ankle.
  "   of head of fibula.
  "   of lower jaw.
  "   of manubrium.
  "   of os calcis.
  "   of patella.
  "   of phalanx.
  "   of sternal end of clavicle.
  "   of vertebra.

5. Diuresis (Diabetes insipidus.)

1. Dolor faucium.

1,4. Dropsy, ovarian.

4. Duodenitis.

5. Durities gingivarum.

4. Dysentery.

4.   "   chronic.

4. Dysmenorrhœa.

4. Dyspepsia, acute.

4.   "   chronic.

3,4,5. Dysuria.

5. Eclampsia.

5.   "   infantum.

6.   "   nutans.

4.   "   puerperal.

1,3. Ecchymosis.

3. Ecthyma.

1. Ectopia lentis.

3. Ectozoa.

        (Pediculus capitis.)

        (    "    vestimenti.)

        (Phthirius inguinalis.)

1. Ectropion.

3. Eczema.

       "    capitis.

       "    chronic.

       "    circinatum.

       "    faciei.

       "    impetiginodes.

            rubrum.

       "    squamosum.

3. Elephantiasis Græcorum.

4. Embolism.

1. Emmetropia.

2. Emphysema, interlobular.

1.    "    of cellular tissue.

2.    "    vesicular.

2. Empyema.

4. Encephalitis.

1. Encephalocele (hernia cerebri.)

2. Endocarditis.

4. Endometritis.

       "    acute.

            chronic cervical.

       "    "    corporeal.

4. Enteralgia.

4. Enteritis.

4. Entozoa.

        (Ascaris lumbricoides.)

        (Bothriocephalus latus.)

        (Oxyuris vermicularis.)

        (Tænia solium.)

5.       (Trichina spiralis.)

1. Entropion.

3. Ephelis.

5. Ephemera.

4.    "     puerperal.

1. Epicanthis.

3. Epididymitis.

5. Epilepsy.

1. Epispadias.

5. Epistaxis.

1. Epulis.

3. Erysipelas of Face.

1.    "     phlegmonous.

3. Erythema.

      "     circinatum.

      "     nodosum.


5. Febricula.

5. Fever.

      "     infantile remittent.

      "     intermittent.

      "     puerperal.

      "     relapsing.

      "     remittent.

2

5. Fever, scarlet, simple.
  "  "  anginose.
  "  "  malignant.
  " typhoid.
  " typhus.
  " yellow.
1. Fissure of anus.
1. " of palate.
1. Fistula, abdominal.
1. " in ano.
1. " lachrymalis.
1. " lymphalis.
1. " salivary.
1,3. " urinary.
1. " vaginal.
1. Flexure of bone.
1. Foreign body in air-passages.
  " " " ear.
  " " " eye.
  " " " nose.
  " " " œsophagus.
  " " " pharynx.
  " " " rectum.
  " " " soft parts.
  " " " urethra.
  " " " vagina.
1. Fracture of acromion.
  " " carpus.
  " " cervix femoris.
  " " clavicle.

1. Fracture of coccyx.
　　　"　　"　cranium.
　　　"　　"　fibula.
　　　"　　"　costal cartilage.
　　　"　　"　inferior maxilla.
　　　"　　"　malar bone.
　　　"　　"　metacarpus.
　　　"　　"　metatarsus.
　　　"　　"　olecranon.
　　　"　　"　os brachii.
　　　"　　"　os femoris.
　　　"　　"　os nasi.
　　　"　　"　patella.
　　　"　　"　pelvis.
　　　"　　"　phalanx.
　　　"　　"　radius.
　　　"　　"　"　and ulna.
　　　"　　"　rib.
　　　"　　"　scapula.
　　　"　　"　spine.
　　　"　　"　sternum.
　　　"　　"　superior maxilla.
　　　"　　"　tarsus.
　　　"　　"　tibia.
　　　"　　"　"　and fibula.
　　　"　　"　ulna.

1. Furunculus.


1. Ganglion.
1,5. Gangrene.

1. Gangrene, traumatic.

4. Gastritis, acute.

4.    "    chronic.

1. Gelatio.

1. Genu-valgum.

1. Gland, enlarged lymphatic.

1. Glaucoma.

1. Glossitis.

5. Gout.

5.    "  rheumatic.

1. Gravedo.

2. Graves' disease.

4. Graviditas.

3. Gumma, syphilitic.


4. Hæmatemesis.

1. Hæmatocele.

4.    "    periuterine.

1.    "    traumatic.

1. Hæmatoma.

3. Hæmaturia.

2. Hæmoptysis.

1. Hæmorrhage.

4.    "    climacteric.

5.    "    from umbilicus.

4,5.    "    intestinal.

4.    "    post partum.

1.    "    traumatic.

1,3.    "    urethral.

4.    "    uterine.

1. Hæmorrhoids.
1,5. Hare-lip.
2. Heart, aneurism of.
2,5. " dilatation of.
2,5. " disease of.
2,5. " enlargement of.
2,5. " fatty disease of.
2,5. " functional disease of.
2,5. " hypertrophy of.
2,5. " malformation of.
2,5. " valve-disease of.
1. Hemeralopia.
4. Hepatitis.
1. Hernia.
  " congenital.
  " femoral.
  " infantile.
  " inguinal.
  " irreducible.
  " pudendal.
  " strangulated.
  " umbilical.
  " vaginal.
3. Herpes.
3. " circinatus.
1. " conjunctivæ.
1. " corneæ.
3. " labialis.
3. " præputialis.
3. " zoster.

1. Hordeolum.

1,2,4,5. Hydatids.

1. Hydrocele.

" congenital.

" encysted.

" of cord.

5. Hydrocephalus (chronic.)

4. Hydrometra.

1. Hydrops articuli.

2. " pericardii.

4. " ovarii.

4. " renum.

1. Hydrosareocele.

2. Hydrothorax.

1,5. Hyperæsthesia of a part.

5. Hypochondriasis.

1. Hypopion.

1. Hypospadias.

5. Hysteria.

4. Icterus.

3. Icthyosis.

4. Ileus.

3. Impetigo.

2. Influenza.

" contagious.

1. Injury of a part.

5. Insanity.

5. Insolation.

1. Iritis.

3. " syphilitic.

1. Irritable stump.

3. Keloid, cicatricial.
3.   "    true.
1. Keratitis.
4. Kidney, congestion of.
4.   "   disease of.

5. Laryngismus stridulus.
1. Laryngitis, acute.
1.    "    chronic.
1.    "    œdematous.
3.    "    syphilitic.
1. Larynx, tumor of.
1. Leucoma.
4. Leucorrhœa, uterine.
4.    "    vaginal.
3. Lichen.
     "   æstivus.
5. Lithiasis.
4. Liver, acute atrophy of.
     "   cirrhosis of.
     "   congestion of.
     "   enlargement of.
     "   fatty.
     "   lardaceous.
5. Locomotor ataxia.
5. Lumbago.
2. Lung, congestion of.
     "   œdema of.

3. Lupus erythematosus.
    "    exedens.
    "    non-exedens.
    "    serpiginosus.
1. Lymphadenitis.
    "    strumous.
    "    traumatic.
1. Lymphangeitis.

1,5. Malformation.
5. Marasmus.
1,4. Mastitis.
4. Mastodynia.
5. Melæna neonatorum.
4,5. Meningitis.
4,5.    "    cerebro-spinal.
5.    "    infantum.
5.    "    spinal.
5.    "    tubercular.
4. Menses, absent.
    "    delayed.
    "    premature cessation of.
    "    retained.
4. Menstruation, excessive.
    "    painful.
    "    premature.
    "    suppressed.
    "    supplementary.
    "    vicarious.
4. Metralgia (uterine colic.)

4. Metritis.

4. " acute.

4. " chronic.

4. " " cervical.

4. " " corporeal.

4. " hæmorrhagic.

4. Miscarriage.

5. Mollities ossium.

3. Molluscum.

3,5. Morbilli.

1. Morbus coxarius.

5. Myalgia.

5. Myelitis.

1. Myopia.


1. Nævus.

1. Necrosis.

4. Nephritis, acute.

4. " chronic.

5. Neuralgia.

5. " facial.

5. " frontal (hemicrania.)

5. " mesenterica (lead colic.)

4. " ovarian.

5. " sciatic.

3. " testis.

1. Nipple, ulcerated.

3. Node.

5. Nostalgia.

1. Nyctalopia.

1. Nystagmus.


4. Obstruction, intestinal.

1.  "  lachrymal.

4,5.  "  of bile-ducts.

4,5.  "  of vena portæ.

1. Œdema.

1.  "  of glottis.

2.  "  " lung.

4. Œsophagitis,

1. Onychia.

1.  "  maligna.

3.  "  syphilitic.

3. Onychomycosis.

1. Onyxis.

3. Ophthalmia, blennorrhagic

1.  "  catarrhal.

1.  "  chronic.

3,5.  "  morbillosa.

5.  "  neonatorum.

1,5  "  purulent.

1.  "  pustular.

3,5.  "  scarlatinosa.

1,5.  "  strumous.

1  "  sympathetic.

3,5.  "  tarsi.

3. Orchitis, blennorrhagic.

3.  "  strumous.

3.  "  syphilitic.

1. Osteitis.

1. Osteo-myelitis.

1. Otitis, acute.

1.    "    chronic.

1,5. Otorrhœa.

4. Ovaritis, acute.

4.    "    chronic.

1. Ozœna.

3.    "    syphilitic.


1. Pannus.

4,5. Paralysis.

5.    "    agitans.

5.    "    diphtherica.

5.    "    facial.

4.    "    (hemiplegia.)

5.    "    infantile.

1,5·    "    local.

1,5.    "    (paraplegia.)

5.    "    saturnine.

1.    "    traumatic.

4. Parametritis.

3. Paraphymosis.

1,3. Paronychia.

4. Parturition.

1. Parulis.

5. Pectus carinatum.

3. Pemphigus.

3,5.    "    neonatorum.

3.    "    syphilitic.

4. Perforation of intestine.

1,3. " " palate.

1. Periarthritis.

2. Pericarditis.

4. Perimetritis.

1. Perineum, lacerated.

1. Periostitis.

1. " syphilitic.

4. Peritonitis.

4. " chronic.

4. " limited.

4. '. pelvic.

1. " traumatic.

4. " tubercular.

5. Pertussis. ·

1,5. Pharyngitis, acute.

1,5. " chronic.

1. Phlebitis.

4. Phlegmasia dolens.

2. Phthisis pulmonalis.

1. Phymosis.

4. Physometra.

3. Pityriasis.

" capitis.

" rubra.

2. Pleurisy, acute.

2. " chronic.

2. Pleurodynia.

2. Pneumonia.

2. " chronic.

2. Pneumonia, lobar.

2,5.   "   lobular (broncho-pnenmonia of children.)

2. Pneumothorax.

5. Poisoning, acute.

5.   "   chronic.

3.   "   local.

1. Polypus.

1.   "   nasi.

4.   "   uteri.

3. Posthitis.

1,5. Pott's disease.

1. Procidentia oculi.

3.   "   tubulorum testis (hernia testis.)

4.   "   uteri.

5. Progressive muscular atrophy.

1. Prostate, chronic enlargement of.

1,3. Prostatitis, acute.

1,3.   "   chronic.

3. Prurigo.

3. Pruritus.

3.   "   ani.

3.   "   vulvæ.

1. Pseudarthrosis,

3. Psoriasis.

1. Pterygium.

4,5. Ptosis.

5. Ptyalism.

2. Pulmonary extravasation.

3. Purpura.

3.   "   hæmorrhagica.

1,5. Pyæmia.

1,5.     "    chronic.

4. Pyelitis.


5. Rachitismus.

1. Ranula.

1. Rectum, prolapse of.

1. Resolutio faucium.

1. Retinitis.

5. Rheumatism, acute articular.

5.     "    chronic.

3.     "    gonorrhœal.

5.     "    muscular.

3,5. Roseola.

3. Rupia syphilitica.

1. Rupture of muscle.

1.     "    " ligamentum patellæ.

1.     "    " perineum.

1.     "    " tendon.


3. Sarcocele.

3.     "    cystic.

3.     "    malignant.

3.     "    strumous.

3.     "    syphilitic.

1,3. Scabies.

3,5. Scleroma.

1. Sclerotitis.

5. Scorbutus.

5. Senectus.

1. Sinus.

5. Spasm, muscular.

3. Spermatorrhœa.

4. Spleen, congestion of.

4.    " hypertrophy of (leucocythæmia.)

4. Splenitis.

1. Spina bifida.

1. Spinal cord, compression of.

1.    " concussion of.

5.    " softening of.

1. Spine, lateral curvature of.

1.    " Pott's disease of.

1. Staphyloma corneæ.

1.    " sclerotic.

1. Strabismus.

1,5. Stomatitis.

1,5.    " gangrenous (canc. oris.)

1,5.    " ulcerative.

1,5.    " vesicular (thrush.)

1. Stremma.

1. Stricture of œsophagus.

1·    " " rectum.

3.    " " urethra.

3,5. Strophulus.

5. Struma.

1. Surditas.

1. Symblepharon.

1. Synechia, anterior.

1,    " posterior.

1. Synovitis, acute.
1. " chronic.
1. " strumous.
1. " traumatic.
3. Syphilis, initial lesion of (hard chancre.)
3. " inguinal adenopathy (following hard chancre.)
3. " inherited.
3. " constitutional, acquired.
3. " (syphilide, macular.)
3. " ( " papular.)
3. " ( " pustular.)
3. " ( " vesicular.)
3. " ( " · " circinate.)
3. " ( " tubercular, grouped.)
3. " ( " " disseminated.)
3. " ( " " ulcerating.)
3. " ( " " serpiginous.)
3. " ( " " pustulo-crustaceous.)


5. Tabes mesenterica.
1. Talipes, calcaneo-valgus.
1. " calcaneus.
1. " equineo-varus.
1. " equineus.
1. " valgus.
1. " varus.
5. Tetanus.
1. Thecitis.
1. Thrombus.

3,5. Tinea decalvans.

3,5.   "   favosa.

3.   "   sycosis.

3,5.   "   tonsurans.

3,5.   "   versicolor.

1. Tonsils, enlarged.

1,5. Torticollis.

5.   "   rheumatic.

1. Trachoma.

5. Tremor, mercurial.

1. Trichiasis.

5. Trichiniasis.

5. Trismus nascentium.

4. Tumor, abdominal.

1.   "   cartilaginous.

1.   "   encysted.

1.   "   fatty.

1.   "   fibro-cellular.

1.   "   fibro-nucleated.

1.   "   fibro-plastic.

1.   "   fibro-vascular.

1,4.   "   fibrous.

1.   "   glandular.

1.   "   myeloid.

1.   "   (neuroma.)

1.   "   osseous.

4.   "   ovarian.

1.   "   recurring fibroid.

1.   "   sarcomatous.

4

1. Tumor, vascular.
3. " " of meatus urinarius.
4. Typhlitis.


1. Ulcer.
1. " chronic.
3. " eczematous.
1. " haemorrhagic.
1. " indolent.
1. " inflamed.
1. " irritable.
1. " of cornea.
1. " of larynx.
4. " of stomach.
3. " rodent.
1. " sloughing.
1. " strumous
1. " varicose.
1. " weak.
4. Ulceration of intestine.
1,5. Ulitis (gingivitis.)
1. Unguis involutus.
1. Urine, extravasation of.
5. " incontinence of.
1,4. " retention of.
4. " suppression of.
3,5. Urticaria.
1. Ustio.

1. Wound of artery.
1.  "  of eye, penetrating.
1.  "  of joint, penetrating.
1,  "  of thorax, penetrating.
1.  "  poisoned.
1.  "  punctured.

# New York Dispensary Standard Non-officinal Preparations.

## TABLE FOR ADJUSTING DOSE TO AGE.

| AGE... | Under 1 year. | 2 years. | 3 years. | 4 years. | 7 years. | 14 years | 21 years. |
|---|---|---|---|---|---|---|---|
| DOSE.. | $\frac{1}{16}$ — $\frac{1}{12}$ | $\frac{1}{8}$ | $\frac{1}{6}$ | $\frac{1}{4}$ | $\frac{1}{3}$ | $\frac{2}{3}$ | 1 |

## LINIMENTA.

LIN. SAPONIS COMP.

| | |
|---|---|
| Saponis Castil. | ℥ x. |
| Ol. Origani | ℥ iv. |
| Alcohol | O.jss. |
| Aquæ. | O.ivss |

LIN. STRAMONII.

| | |
|---|---|
| Ung. Stramonii. | ℥ ij. |
| Liq. Plumb. Subac. | ℥ j. |
| Ol. Lini. | ℥ viij. |

LIN. IODINII COMP.

| | |
|---|---|
| Iodinii | gr. x. |
| Potass. Iodidi | ℥ ss. |
| Sodii Chlor. | ℥ ij. |
| Aquæ | O.ij. |

# New York Dispensary Standard Non-officinal Preparations.

TABLE FOR ADJUSTING DOSE TO AGE.

| AGE... | Under 1 year. | 2 years. | 3 years. | 4 years. | 7 years. | 14 years | 21 years. |
|--------|---------------|----------|----------|----------|----------|----------|-----------|
| DOSE.. | $\frac{1}{15} - \frac{1}{12}$ | $\frac{1}{8}$ | $\frac{1}{6}$ | $\frac{1}{4}$ | $\frac{1}{3}$ | $\frac{2}{3}$ | $1$ |

32

# New York Dispensary Standard Non-officinal Preparations.

### TABLE FOR ADJUSTING DOSE TO AGE.

| AGE... | Under 1 year. | 2 years. | 3 years. | 4 years. | 7 years. | 14 years | 21 years. |
|---|---|---|---|---|---|---|---|
| Dose .. | $\frac{1}{15} - \frac{1}{12}$ | $\frac{1}{8}$ | $\frac{1}{6}$ | $\frac{1}{4}$ | $\frac{1}{3}$ | $\frac{2}{3}$ | 1 |

## PULVERES.

PULV. BISMUTH. ET OPII.

Bismuth. Subnitrat ................................... gr. v'
Pulv. Opii............................. .......... gr. j.
Pulv. Acaciæ........................................ gr. x.

PULV. SENNÆ COMP.

Pulv. Sennæ,
Potass. Bitartrat,
Pulv. Sulphuris, āā................................... ℥ ij.
Pulv. Zingiberis....................................... ℥ ·s.

PULV. ZINCI COMP.

Zinci Oxidi,
Hyd. Chlo. Mit., āā................................... ℈ j.
Pulv. Amyli......................................... ℈ ij.
(For external use.)

PULV. OPII ALKALIN.

Pulv. Opii....... ................................ gr. ss.
Sod. et Pot. Tart............................. ............. ℈ j.
Potass. Bicarb....................................... gr. x.

# New York Dispensary Standard Non-officinal Preparations.

TABLE FOR ADJUSTING DOSE TO AGE.

| AGE... | Under 1 year. | 2 years. | 3 years. | 4 years. | 7 years. | 14 years. | 21 years. |
|---|---|---|---|---|---|---|---|
| DOSE .. | $\frac{1}{15}$ — $\frac{1}{12}$ | $\frac{1}{8}$ | $\frac{1}{6}$ | $\frac{1}{4}$ | $\frac{1}{3}$ | $\frac{2}{3}$ | 1 |

# New York Dispensary Standard Non-officinal Preparations.

## TABLE FOR ADJUSTING DOSE TO AGE.

| AGE... | Under 1 year. | 2 years. | 3 years. | 4 years. | 7 years. | 14 years | 21 years. |
|---|---|---|---|---|---|---|---|
| DOSE.. | $\frac{1}{16}$—$\frac{1}{12}$ | $\frac{1}{8}$ | $\frac{1}{6}$ | $\frac{1}{4}$ | $\frac{1}{3}$ | $\frac{2}{3}$ | 1 |

## LOTIONES.

LOT. EVAP.

Ammoniæ Muriat.,

Potass. Nitrat., āā..................................... ℥ ij.

Alcohol .............................................. O.jss.

Aquæ................................................ O.iv.

LOT. FERRI.

Ferri et Potass. Tart................................. ℥ ss.

Aquæ................................................ O.j.

LOT. FLAVA.

Hyd. Chlo. Corros................................... gr. j.

Liq. Calcis ......................................... ℥ j.

LOT. NIGRA.

Hyd. Chlo. Mit...................................... ℈ ij.

Liq. Calcis ......................................... O. j.

LOT. RUBRA.

Zinci Sulph........................................gr. xlviij.

Sp. Lav. Comp...................................... ℥ j.

Aquæ...... ......................................... O.j.

LOT. PLUMBI ET OPII.

Liq. Plumb. Subac ................................. ℈ ij.

Tinct. Opii......................................... ℥ j.

Aquæ............................................... O.j.

LOT. BORACIS.

Sodæ Biborat ...................................... gr. x.

Aquæ Camph....................................... ℥ j.

# New York Dispensary Standard Non-officinal Preparations.

## TABLE FOR ADJUSTING DOSE TO AGE.

| AGE... | Under 1 year. | 2 years. | 3 years. | 4 years. | 7 years. | 14 years | 21 years. |
|---|---|---|---|---|---|---|---|
| DOSE.. | $\frac{1}{15}$ — $\frac{1}{12}$ | $\frac{1}{8}$ | $\frac{1}{6}$ | $\frac{1}{4}$ | $\frac{1}{3}$ | $\frac{2}{3}$ | 1 |

LOT. SOD. CHLORINAT.

Liq. Sod. Chlorin...................................... ℥ ss.

Aquæ............................................... ℥ iijss.

LOT. ACIDI CARBOL.

Ac. Carbol. Cryst..................................... ℨ ij.

Aquæ............................................... ℥ viij.

de#g36

# New York Dispensary Standard Non-officinal Preparations.

## TABLE FOR ADJUSTING DOSE TO AGE.

| AGE... | Under 1 year. | 2 years. | 3 years. | 4 years. | 7 years. | 14 years | 21 years. |
|---|---|---|---|---|---|---|---|
| DOSE.. | $\frac{1}{15} - \frac{1}{12}$ | $\frac{1}{8}$ | $\frac{1}{6}$ | $\frac{1}{4}$ | $\frac{1}{3}$ | $\frac{2}{3}$ | 1 |

# PILULÆ.

PIL. ALOËS ET FERRI.
Ferri Sulph.,
Pulv. Aloës,
Ext. Gentian, āā ........................................ gr. 1¾.

PIL. HYDRARG. PROTIODID.
Hydrarg. Protiodid........ ............................ gr. ¼
Ext. Gentian.
Pulv. Glycyrrhiz, āā ............................. ......... gr. j.

PIL. PLUMBI ET OPII.
Plumbi Acetat........................................ .... gr. j.
Pulv. Opii..................... ......................... gr. ⅛
Pulv. Glycyrrhiz ........................................ gr. ½
Syr. Simp........................................ .......... q.s.

PIL. TRIPLEX.
Pulv. Aloës,
Ext. Colocynth. Comp.,
Pil. Hydrarg., āā.... . .............. .............. ...... gr. j.
Syr. Simp ............................................. q. s.

PIL. NUC. VOMIC. COMP.
Ext. Nuc. Vomic............................. ............ gr. ss.
Pulv. Scammonii ...................... ............... gr. j.
Pulv. Aloës,
Pulv. Rhei, āā ......................................... gr. ¾
Alcohol ............................. .................... q. s.

# New York Dispensary Standard Non-officinal Preparations.

## TABLE FOR ADJUSTING DOSE TO AGE.

| AGE... | Under 1 year. | 2 years. | 3 years. | 4 years. | 7 years. | 14 years | 21 years. |
|---|---|---|---|---|---|---|---|
| DOSE.. | $\frac{1}{15} - \frac{1}{12}$ | $\frac{1}{8}$ | $\frac{1}{6}$ | $\frac{1}{4}$ | $\frac{1}{3}$ | $\frac{2}{3}$ | $1$ |

PIL. (DUPUYTREN.)

Hydrarg. Chlo. Corros.................................... gr. $\frac{1}{8}$

Pulv. Guaiaci... ............................ ............. gr. $2\frac{1}{2}$

Ext. Conii............................................ gr. $\frac{5}{6}$

PIL PODOPHYLLIN. COMP.

Podophyllinæ........................................ gr. ss.

Leptandrinæ........................................ gr. j.

Ext. Taraxaci....................................... q. s.

# New York Dispensary Standard Non-officinal Preparations.

## TABLE FOR ADJUSTING DOSE TO AGE.

| AGE... | Under 1 year. | 2 years. | 3 years. | 4 years. | 7 years. | 14 years | 21 years. |
|---|---|---|---|---|---|---|---|
| DOSE.. | $\frac{1}{15}$ — $\frac{1}{12}$ | $\frac{1}{8}$ | $\frac{1}{6}$ | $\frac{1}{4}$ | $\frac{1}{3}$ | $\frac{2}{3}$ | 1 |

## PIGMENTA.

PIG. ACACIÆ COMP.

Pulv. Acaciæ ........................................... ℥ iij.

Pulv. Tragacanth................................... ℥ j.

Syr. Fusci... .......................................... ℥ iv.

Aquæ Calidæ........................................ ℥ xij.

PIG. SAPONIS VIRIDIS.

Saponis Viridis,

Alcoholis, partes æquales.

PIG. SAPONIS VIRID. COMP.

Saponis Viridis,

Ol. Cadini,

Alcoholis, partes æquales.

## SOLUTIONES.

POTASS. IOD................................................gr. x— ℥ j.

QUIN. SULPH.........................................  ......gr. ij— ℥ j.

POTASS. BROMID..................................  ............. ℨ ss— ℥ j.

ZINC. SULPH..............................................gr. ij— ℥ j.

POTASS. CHLO............................................ (ad sat.)

# New York Dispensary Standard Non-officinal Preparations.

## TABLE FOR ADJUSTING DOSE TO AGE.

| AGE... | Under 1 year. | 2 years. | 3 years. | 4 years. | 7 years. | 14 years. | 21 years. |
|---|---|---|---|---|---|---|---|
| DOSE .. | $\frac{1}{15}$ — $\frac{1}{12}$ | $\frac{1}{8}$ | $\frac{1}{6}$ | $\frac{1}{4}$ | $\frac{1}{3}$ | $\frac{2}{3}$ | 1 |

# New York Dispensary Standard Non-officinal Preparations.

## TABLE FOR ADJUSTING DOSE TO AGE.

| AGE... | Under 1 year. | 2 years. | 3 years. | 4 years. | 7 years. | 14 years | 21 years. |
|---|---|---|---|---|---|---|---|
| DOSE.. | $\frac{1}{16}-\frac{1}{12}$ | $\frac{1}{8}$ | $\frac{1}{6}$ | $\frac{1}{4}$ | $\frac{1}{3}$ | $\frac{2}{3}$ | $1$ |

# GARGARISMATA.

GARG. ALUMINIS.

    Aluminis.

    Potass. Chlorat, āā........ . .........................     ℈ j.

    Aquæ...............................................     O.ss.

GARG. ACID. TANNIC.

    Acid. Tannic.... ....................................·     ℨ ss

    Glycerinæ...........................................       ℈ ij.

    Aquæ Camph.... .................. ..............         ℥ vj.

# UNGUENTA.

UNG. SULPH. ALKALIN, (HELMERICH.)

    Sulphur. Sublim....................................     ℥ ij.

    Potass. Carbonat........... ......................     ℥ j.

    Adipis ........... . ...........................     ℥ viij.

UNG. ACIDI CARBOL.

    Ac. Carbol. Cryst...................................     ℈ ss.

    Ung. Adipis .... ............. ...............     ℥ j.

UNG. BALS. PERU.

    Bals. Peru... .......................................     ℈ j.

    Ung. Resinæ.......................................     ℥ j

# New York Dispensary Standard Non-officinal Preparations.

## TABLE FOR ADJUSTING DOSE TO AGE.

| AGE... | Under 1 year. | 2 years. | 3 years. | 4 years. | 7 years. | 14 years. | 21 years. |
|---|---|---|---|---|---|---|---|
| DOSE.. | $\frac{1}{15}$ — $\frac{1}{12}$ | $\frac{1}{8}$ | $\frac{1}{6}$ | $\frac{1}{4}$ | $\frac{1}{3}$ | $\frac{2}{3}$ | 1 |

# New York Dispensary Standard Non-officinal Preparations.

## TABLE FOR ADJUSTING DOSE TO AGE.

| AGE... | Under 1 year. | 2 years. | 3 years. | 4 years. | 7 years. | 14 years | 21 years. |
|---|---|---|---|---|---|---|---|
| DOSE.. | $\frac{1}{16}$—$\frac{1}{12}$ | $\frac{1}{8}$ | $\frac{1}{6}$ | $\frac{1}{4}$ | $\frac{1}{3}$ | $\frac{2}{3}$ | 1 |

## MISTURÆ.

| | | In each Tea-spoonful. | In each Table-spoonful. |
|---|---|---|---|
| MIST. POT. ET HYOSCY. | | | |
| Potass. Bicarb.................. | ℥ j. | 7 grs. | 27 grs. |
| Tinct. Hyosc................... | ℥ ss. | 3½ m. | 15 m. |
| Aquæ....................... ...... | O.ss. | | |
| MIST. COPAIBÆ. | | | |
| Bals. Copaibæ... ............... | ℥ iij. | 6 m. | 22 m. |
| Liq. Potassæ...... ............ | ℥ iv. | 7 m. | 30 m. |
| Aqu. Anisi.................... | ℥ iij. | | |
| Syr. Simpl........ | ℥ ij. | | |
| MIST. OL. MORRHUÆ. | | | |
| Ol. Morrhuæ.................. | ℥ iij. | 25 m. | 100 m. |
| Syr. Pruni Virg., | | | |
| Liq. Calcis, āā,................. | ℥ j. | 9 m. | 34 m. |
| MIST. RHEI ET SODÆ. | | | |
| Pulv. Rhei, | | | |
| Sodæ Bicarb., āā................ | ℥ ij. | 1 gr. | 4 gr. |
| Aq. Menth. Pip................. | O.v. | | |
| MIST. STOMACHIC. | | | |
| Sodæ Bicarb.................... | ℥ j. | 1 gr. | 4 gr. |
| Tinct. Cardamom. Comp., | | | |
| Tinct. Gentian. Comp., āā ........ | ℥ ij. | 2 m. | 8 m. |
| Aq. Menth. Pip................. | O.iij. | | |

# New York Dispensary Standard Non-officinal Preparations.

## TABLE FOR ADJUSTING DOSE TO AGE.

| AGE... | Under 1 year. | 2 years. | 3 years. | 4 years. | 7 years. | 14 years. | 21 years. |
|---|---|---|---|---|---|---|---|
| DOSE.. | $\frac{1}{15}$—$\frac{1}{12}$ | $\frac{1}{8}$ | $\frac{1}{6}$ | $\frac{1}{4}$ | $\frac{1}{3}$ | $\frac{2}{3}$ | 1 |

**MIST. COLCHICI.**

| | | | |
|---|---|---|---|
| Potass. Iodid..................... | ℈ij. | 1¼ gr. | 5 gr. |
| Ext. Colchici Acet............... | gr. viij· | ¼ gr. | 1 gr. |
| Ext. Hyoscyami ............... .. | gr. xvj. | ½ gr. | 2 gr. |
| Aquæ.......................... | ℥ iv. | | |

**MIST. DIURETIC.**

| | | | |
|---|---|---|---|
| Sp. Æth. Nit.......... ·......... | ℥ ss. | 12 m. | 48 m. |
| Liq. Ammon. Ac., | | | |
| Infus. Buchu, āā ............ ..... | ℥ j. | 24 m. | 96 m. |

**MIST. POT. ACETAT.**

| | | | |
|---|---|---|---|
| Pot. Acetat..................... | ℨ iij. | 18 gr. | 72 gr. |
| Vin. Colch. Rad................. | ℨ ij. | 12 m. | 48 m. |
| Aqu. Menth. Pip................ | ℥ iv. | | |

**MIST. GLYCYRRHIZ.**

| | | | |
|---|---|---|---|
| Ext. Ipecac. Fl.................. | ℨ ss | ¼ m. | 1 m. |
| Ext. Glycyrrhiz ................. | ℥ j. | 4 gr. | 15 gr. |
| Aqu. Camph.................... | ℥ xv. | | |

**MIST. EXPECTOR.**

(For children.)

| | | | |
|---|---|---|---|
| Tr. Opii Camph... ............. | ℥ ij. | 4 m. | 16 m. |
| Ext. Ipecac. Fl................. | ℨ j. | ¼ m. | 1 m. |
| Syr. Tolu...................... | ℥ xxviij. | | |

**MIST. EXPECT. (STOKES.)**

| | | | |
|---|---|---|---|
| Tinct. Opii Camph.............. | ℨ ij. | 2¼ m. | 10 m. |
| Ammon. Carb................. | ℈j. | ⅓ gr. | 1⅓ gr. |
| Tinct. Scillæ.................... | ℨ ij. | 2½ m. | 10 m. |
| Syr. Tolu..................... | ℥ ss. | | |
| Decoct. Senegæ................ | ℥ v. | 50 m. | 200 m. |

# New York Dispensary Standard Non-officinal Preparations.

## TABLE FOR ADJUSTING DOSE TO AGE.

| AGE... | Under 1 year. | 2 years. | 3 years. | 4 years. | 7 years. | 14 years. | 21 years. |
|---|---|---|---|---|---|---|---|
| DOSE.. | $\frac{1}{15} - \frac{1}{12}$ | $\frac{1}{8}$ | $\frac{1}{6}$ | $\frac{1}{4}$ | $\frac{1}{3}$ | $\frac{2}{3}$ | 1 |

MIST. RHEI ET OPII.

    Tr. Opii Camph,,

    Tr. Rhei Comp., āā.. ............    ℥ ss.    15 m.    60 m.

    Aquæ.........................    ℥ j.

MIST. CRETÆ COMP.

    Tr. Opii Camph.,

    Tr. Catechu, āā.................    ℈ ij.    4 m.    16 m.

    Mist. Cretæ....................    ℥ iijss.

MIST. FERRI ET QUINIÆ.

    Tr. Ferri Chlor.................    ℈ ij.    4 m.    16 m.

    Quiniæ Sulph..................    gr.xvj.    $\frac{1}{2}$ gr.    2 gr.

    Aquæ.........................    ℥ iv.

MIST. HYDRARG. BINIODID.

    Hydrarg. Biniodid ..............    gr.j.    1-32 gr.    $\frac{1}{4}$ gr.

    Potass. Iodidi ..................    ℥ ss.    7$\frac{1}{2}$ gr.    30 gr.

    Infus. Gent. Comp .............    v ℥ i.

# New York Dispensary Standard Non-officinal Preparations.

## TABLE FOR ADJUSTING DOSE TO AGE.

| AGE... | Under 1 year. | 2 years. | 3 years. | 4 years. | 7 years. | 14 years | 21 years. |
|---|---|---|---|---|---|---|---|
| DOSE.. | $\frac{1}{15} - \frac{1}{12}$ | $\frac{1}{8}$ | $\frac{1}{6}$ | $\frac{1}{4}$ | $\frac{1}{3}$ | $\frac{2}{3}$ | $1$ |